Lawns & Mowers

Lawncare for *novice* gardeners

ISBN: 978-1-8382287-0-5

Lawns & Mowers

Lawncare for *novice* gardeners

Martin Sallai

Contents

Foreword

Many people believe that there is nothing more aesthetically pleasing than the undulation of a neat, healthy, and beautifully manicured lawn. However, you need to invest great amounts of time, effort and dedication to establish and maintain a successful lawn.

I have spent years as a part-time gardener and blogger. Over these years I have gained experience in lawn care and maintenance and learnt a great deal about the do's and don'ts of gardening in general. The following are the two most valuable lessons that I have learnt:

Firstly, a good lawn takes time, it can take many years for a lawn to become the beautiful one that you should be aiming for, but it will get there eventually.

Secondly, 'to make an omelette you have got to break some eggs'. If you start carrying out these maintenance tasks your lawn is likely to look worse before it looks better. If this is the case, you should persevere and bear in mind that it will get better.

Whilst many lawncare books and publications offer guidance in detailed technical terminology, not many offer a simple guide for beginners. With this book I aim to help hobby gardeners and individuals with limited lawn care experience, to gain a good understanding of what is needed to establish and maintain a good quality domestic lawn. You do not need years of experience to create a beautiful lawn, but some advice may help on how to carry out routine lawncare tasks, how to select the appropriate lawn care equipment and how to use the equipment effectively.

In this guide, I will be walking you through how to achieve and maintain the characteristics of a healthy and successful lawn. I will also be giving general tips and guidance on how to go about routine gardening tasks such as mowing, fertilising, and scarifying. This should help to transform amateur hobby gardeners into developing experts in lawn care.

There are many different types of lawn: from the typical back garden lawn to a wildlife meadow to majestic parkland turf. I will be explaining how to maintain a good, healthy lawn regardless of what type it may be. I will be offering advice on a range of lawn care topics from how to establish a lawn to achieving those legendary stripes. Hopefully, you will find my tips useful no matter what your specific lawn requirements may be.

To be successful your lawn must have the following characteristics:

- Adequate thickness and consistency
- Adequate length
- Neatly edged borders
- Lack of unsavoury weeds and bare patches

Chapter one

What you need

In this chapter, I will be advising on different pieces of garden equipment and machinery you may require. I will explore the advantages or disadvantages of them and discuss what to consider when choosing the right one for you. Most of the equipment in this chapter can be acquired from hardware shops, garden centres, and

internet retailers. Well-known brands are likely to produce more reliable machines. While they may be more costly than smaller, less well-known brands, they are likely to last longer and produce a better result. If you are planning to purchase a particularly expensive piece of machinery, such as a lawnmower, I would recommend that you visit a shop or showroom where you can see the machine before purchasing. This will help to ensure that you purchase a machine that is suitable for your requirements. Some large pieces of machinery, such as scarifiers, can also be hired from machinery hire companies; so, if you only need a specialist machine for an annual task, you may wish to consider hiring one.

Lawnmowers

Whatever shape or size your lawn maybe, you need to choose the right lawnmower for your requirements. It is worth considering factors such as whether you require a walk-behind or a ride-on lawnmower, whether you need an electric, petrol, or diesel machine and what cutting width would be most suitable for your requirements. Mowing a lawn should not take much longer than one hour; the wider the cutting width the quicker you get the job done. You should also consider whether you wish to have a collecting, mulching, or discharge lawnmower. I explain these further in the 'Dealing with grass clippings' section of chapter seven.

For gardens that are smaller than half an acre, I would recommend petrol, or electric, walk-behind lawnmower and for gardens that are larger than half an acre, I would recommend a ride-on mower. Even within these categories, there are many different types to choose from. For example, walk-behind lawnmowers are available in both push-along and self-propelled models and ride-on mowers are available in rear-engine, mid-mount, out-front and zero-turn models. Some brands also manufacture cylinder lawnmowers. These are lawnmowers with multiple blades incorporated into horizontal cylinders that rotate against a fixed blade to cut the grass. These types are available in models with anywhere between one and six cylinders, with both walk-behind and ride-on models. In my experience, many cylinder mowers can be incredibly challenging and expensive to maintain and are only really beneficial if used on an immaculate commercial lawn such as a cricket pitch.

Most domestic lawnmowers, however, are rotary ones. Rotary lawn-mowers have standard rotating lawnmower blades located in the cutting deck[1]. They usually have one but can have up to three rotary blades in the cutting deck; it is usually one if it is a walk-behind model and two or three if it is a ride-on mower. I will not be addressing cylinder lawnmow-ers as I believe that for domestic lawns rotary lawnmowers are far more effective. They require less skill on the operator's behalf and are consider-ably more affordable, both to purchase and to maintain. Similarly, I will not be addressing robotic or hover lawnmowers, as in my experience many of them are less than ideal for maintaining medium to large lawns; they can be rather unreliable and/or ineffective even on small lawns. If you have a particularly small lawn you could use a hand-driven cylinder lawnmower, however, I would still recommend using an electric rotary one. Hand-driven lawnmowers are often flimsy and end up tearing the grass blades[2] rather than cutting them (this can cause brown tips on the grass blades). They are also ineffective at collecting grass clippings.

If you have a lawn that is smaller than a quarter of an acre, it is fine to use an electric lawnmower. These are usually the models with the smallest cutting decks. Electric lawnmowers are usually made up of mostly plastic components and are available with both corded and cordless versions. The consensus amongst domestic gardeners is that cordless electric lawnmowers are suitable for small lawns but may struggle with producing sufficient power for obstacles such as bumps or tall grass. Corded electric mowers tend to be more powerful and can be used for

Hand-driven lawnmower

an unlimited amount of time, however, they come with the disadvantage of the operator having to take care not to mow over, or get tangled up in, the power cable. Contrastingly, battery-powered electric lawnmowers have the advantage of the operator not having to deal with a power cable but come with other disadvantages: many models having a very short run time, machines being less reliable and the batteries having to be replaced after a certain number of years. A disadvantage of all-electric lawnmowers is that they can be very dangerous if used in moist conditions, but then you should not be mowing a moist lawn anyway.

For individuals with medium-sized gardens (between 0.25 and 0.5 acres), I would recommend a petrol walk-behind model.

These machines are, in my experience, more powerful and often more reliable than electric ones. Petrol lawnmowers also come in a wide range of cutting widths. They range from relatively small pull-start, push-along models to large electric-start, self-propelled ones; some even feature cup holders. If you have a relatively flat lawn on level ground, you should be fine to use a push-along model; this is the most basic type of lawnmower. It does what it says on the tin; it consists of a basic body with an engine and a cutting blade on it. If your lawn is slightly larger or has steep slopes or banks, you may wish to consider using a self-propelled lawnmower. These lawnmowers are incredibly useful; all you have to do is engage the self-propelled function and walk behind the machine steering it.

Electric walk-behind lawnmower (battery)

Petrol walk-behind lawnmower

Now there is no need to struggle with pushing a heavy lawnmower around the garden.

If you have a garden that is half an acre or larger, I would recommend using a ride-on mower. Ride-on mowers are known as any of the following: ride-on mower, riding-mower, sit-on mower, lawn tractor, and garden tractor. Although there are some technical differences between these names, the relevant part is that the operator is meant to sit in a seat that is affixed to a machine with a cutting deck that is suitable for cutting grass.

Therefore, in this book, I will be referring to all of the above as ride-on mowers. Some small ride-on mowers are simply designed to cut grass and cannot be used for any other purpose. Whereas many medium and large-sized ride-on mowers either come with or have an optional tow-bar for towing small attachments such as trailers, lawn rollers and spreaders. These medium and large-sized models are the ones that I would most recommend, simply because they are extremely versatile and can be used to carry out a wide range of garden tasks. As I have mentioned, there are many different types of ride-on mower.

The smallest type of ride-on mower is a rear-engine model (sometimes referred to as a garden-rider) where the operator's seat is positioned in front of or on top of the engine. The cutting deck, with usually one large blade, is underneath the machine. These machines are designed purely to cut grass; if your lawn is less than an acre in size and you just wish to cut the grass with this machine, it is quite suit-able. However, it is worth noting that these machines usually have the weakest engines of the range and therefore many of them do not offer a tow-bar option. If you wish to tow attachments such as a lawn roller around the garden, you will need to use another machine.

Rear engine ride-on mower

A mid-mount ride-on mower is where the operator's seat is po-sitioned behind the engine, and in front of the grass box (if it has one). This is the most common type of ride-on mower and what is often referred to as a lawn tractor, or garden tractor, due to its shape being somewhat similar to a compact tractor. Whilst on this topic, it is worth noting that there is some dif-ference between a lawn tractor and a garden tractor: a lawn tractor is a medium-sized ride-on mower, usually with an air-cooled engine; it is suitable for towing small attachments such a small trailer or lawn roller. A garden tractor is a larger more heavy-duty machine, usually with a

Mid-mount ride-on mower

liquid-cooled engine. It is capable of towing heavier attachments and in some cases may also be suitable for operating powered attachments. A mid-mount ride-on-mower is suitable for mowing lawns anywhere between half an acre and four acres, they can have anywhere between one and three cutting blades and cutting widths up to sixty inches (there are different models for different lawn sizes). These machines are also very easy to operate (similar to driving a car) and extremely versatile, due to their ability to tow a range of garden attachments.

Out-front ride-on mowers are machines with a cutting deck that is positioned in front of the main machine unit. They offer excellent manoeuvrability with the position of the cutting deck as well as the fact that most of them are articulated models. Some have four-wheel steering and four-wheel drive; they are therefore great for mowing lawns with tight spaces and/or obstacles such as flowerbeds. These ride-on mowers usually have two or three cutting blades and are ideal for lawns anywhere between one and four acres in size (there are different models for different lawn sizes). However, these machines are less suitable for bumpy lawns and due to the articulation, they are also more challenging to operate. Many of these machines do feature tow-bars for towing garden attachments however, it is considerably more challenging to tow an attachment with an articulated machine. Consequently, you have to be a very skilled driver to reverse one of these machines while it is towing an attachment, otherwise, you will frequently find yourself 'jack-knifing'.

Outfront ride-on mower

A zero-turn ride-on mower gets its name from the fact that it has a zero-centimetre turning circle. It can, therefore, perform 180 (or 360) degree turns in the lawn without you having to bother with a three-point turn at the end of the strip of lawn that you are mowing. This advantage in manoeuvrability means that similarly to an out-front ride-on mower, this machine is ideal for mowing lawns with obstacles such as flowerbeds. In recent years more and more individuals from the domestic as well as the commercial sector are opting for zero-turns over mid mount machines.

Zero-turn ride-on mower

This is because the zero-turns' ability to make 180 degree turns quickly and effectively means that larger areas of grass can be cut more efficiently. However, due to the small front wheels and the majority of the weight being positioned at the rear; this machine is less ideal for mowing lawns with bumps, steep slopes, or banks in them.

Many of these machines do not have steering wheels and instead are operated by control levers. As such they require more skill to operate. Although many of them also feature a tow bar, these machines are not as good for towing attachments as standard mid-mount machines.

Additional factors to consider when choosing a ride-on mower include engine size, number of cylinders in the engine, fuel type, whether it is two or four-wheel drive and the ability to mow in reverse.

Small and medium-sized ride-on mowers usually feature a single-cylinder petrol engine; these are quite reliable and will give the machine

Rear PTO

the ability to effectively mow a relatively level lawn. They will tow a relatively light attachment. However, if your lawn has any steep slopes or banks, or you wish to tow a heavy attachment such as a large trailer; you should consider choosing a ride-on mower with a so-called V-twin engine. A V-twin engine is similar to a normal single cylinder ride-on mower engine, but due to having two cylinders, it is just that bit more powerful. This means that it will make quick work of driving up steep slopes or towing heavy attachments.

Powered grass collector

Most ride-on mowers run on either petrol or diesel, however, for individuals who wish to take a more environmentally friendly approach, certain brands do manufacture battery-powered electric ride-on mowers. Whilst these machines are suitable for cutting grass, they can be considerably less powerful than petrol or diesel versions and many of them are therefore unsuitable for towing heavy attachments. Another disadvantage to electric ride-on mowers is that like most battery-powered machines, the batteries can deteriorate over time and need to be replaced after a certain number of years. Some large commercial grade ride-on mowers also offer a diesel engine, which in my experience is the most powerful one of them all.

On some machines the grass sweeper cassette can be swapped out for other attachments such as a scarifier cassette

Whilst most ride-on mowers only feature a mid-Power Take-off (PTO[3]), which operates the cutting deck, certain brands come with both a mid- and a rear PTO. Having a rear PTO means that the machine can operate a range of purpose-made, belt-driven, powered attachments such as a powered grass collector, broadcast spreader and scarifier, both alongside and separate from the cutting deck. I whole-heartedly recommend using one of these machines as they are incredibly versatile and suitable for so many garden tasks.

If you have steep slopes or banks in your garden, you should also consider using a four-wheel-drive ride-on mower. Most ride-on mowers are rear-wheel-drive models; however, many brands do offer at least one four-wheel-drive model. This provides the machine with better traction and will make using the machine on slopes or banks considerably easier and safer.

Some ride-on mowers also offer anti-scalping deck[4] wheels; these are small, usually plastic, wheels or rollers affixed to the cutting deck. They prevent the cutting deck from getting too close to the ground and consequently scalping the lawn.

Another, less significant factor to consider for people who are choosing a ride-on mower is that not all makes and models offer the ability to mow whilst the machine is in reverse. With some makes or models, if the cutting blades are engaged and the machine is put into reverse - as a safety measure - the engine will cut out. The idea behind this is that if the operator was reversing the machine without taking sufficient care, having the cutting blades engaged may cause injury to other individuals in the garden. Whilst this is a perfectly reasonable precaution to take, not having the ability to mow whilst in reverse can make the machine operator's task surprisingly difficult. Therefore, I would recommend opting for a machine that can mow in reverse, and as a safety precaution, ensuring that there are no people or animals apart from the operator in the vicinity of the lawn whilst the machine is in use.

If you intend to create stripes on your lawn, using a lawnmower with an incorporated roller is very helpful. On walk-behind models of such lawnmowers rather than having two rear wheels, the lawnmower

Rear roller on a walk behind lawn mower

just has a roller; this means that with the weight of the lawnmower pushing down on it, the roller bends the grass blades in the direction that the machine is mowing, causing stripes to appear. On some models of ride-on mower, there is a roller attached either to the back of the cutting deck or to the grass collector, this creates the same effect as the rear roller on a walk-behind lawnmower. Striping kits are also available as accessories for certain brands of lawnmowers.

Finally, a factor worth considering irrespective of what type of lawnmower you are choosing is having a deck washout port. A deck washout port is a hose-pipe connector on the cutting deck that a standard garden hose-pipe can be connected to. The aim of this is for you to be able to thoroughly clean the inside of the cutting deck on your lawnmower with minimal effort.

You simply connect a hose-pipe to the washout port on the cutting deck, ensure that the water is running, turn the cutting blades on for a couple of minutes, then disconnect the hose-pipe and the process is finished. Running the cutting deck for a couple of minutes after the water has been turned off helps to dry the inside of the deck, preventing rust. Carrying out this task after having used the lawnmower will ensure that any moist grass clippings, which have stuck

Washout port on a walk behind lawn mower

to the inside of the cutting deck are washed out, thus ensuring that the cutting deck does not start to rust due to the grass clippings.

Strimmer

If you need a lawnmower you are also likely to need a strimmer. Strimmers may also be referred to as grass trimmers, but for this purpose, I will be referring to all of them as strimmers. This is so that you can keep the grass on the borders just as neatly cut as the rest of the lawn. Having overgrown borders can make an entire lawn appear messy and neglected. Most strimmers have either a plastic wire or small plastic blades that spin around at a high speed to cut the grass, some larger machines may also have metal blades or discs to cut the grass. Similarly, to lawnmowers, there are many different makes and sizes of strimmer with different capabilities.

For lawns that are smaller than half an acre, it is suitable to use an electric strimmer; these are available in both corded and cordless models; each has its advantages and disadvantages. Like lawnmowers, a corded electric strimmer is likely to be more powerful than a battery-powered one and can be used for an unlimited amount of time; disadvantages, however, include, the operator is limited by the length of cord and having to take care not to cut or damage the cord. A cordless strimmer has the advantages of not requiring a power supply near to where it is being used and the operator not having to be concerned about cutting the electrical cord; disadvantages, however, include: the machine being less powerful than a corded model, and the run time is limited.

Electric strimmer

Petrol strimmer

If your garden is larger than half an acre or has any banks that are unsuitable for a lawnmower to be used on, you should consider using a petrol strimmer. These machines are more powerful than electric models and are available in both two and four-stroke versions. I would recommend using a four-stroke, as they are known to be more reliable than two-stroke engines. If you are using a four-stroke model, you can also use the same unleaded petrol that you may use in a petrol lawnmower without having to spend time adding the oil to it. Overall, petrol strimmers are very useful as they can be used for an unlimited amount of time, with no requirement for a power source nearby. As I have mentioned, most petrol strimmers can also have a variety of cutting means other than a plastic wire; some of them have metal discs, blades or plates, which are very helpful when cutting through thick grass or weeds (these do require a lot of care to be taken by the operator, as these cutting means can be dangerous if used irresponsibly).

Finally, some petrol strimmers can also be used as multi-tools with purpose-made attachments such as a hedge cutter or chain saw.

If you have a lot of steep banks in your garden that need strimming, you may wish to use a wheeled-trimmer (a walk-behind strimmer). This machine uses the same cutting method as a handheld strimmer – but due to the wheels, you can spend hours cutting without getting a backache.

Lawn edger

Long-handled edging shears

If you wish to maintain a well-manicured lawn, you will need to have well-edged borders. There are many different tools for the task of lawn edging, these include a lawn edging tool, long-handled lawn edging shears, and a petrol or electric lawn edger. You should decide which piece of equipment you wish to use based on the length of the borders of the lawn that need to be edged, how much time you are prepared to spend carrying out this task and how much physical labour you are prepared to undertake.

If you have a relatively small number of borders that need to be edged, you should use a lawn edging tool or long-handled lawn edging shears. A lawn edging tool is a rather simple one that may look somewhat similar to a small spade; this can be used to carve chunks of soil and grass off the edges of the lawn, making it look neat. Long-handled lawn edging shears, on the other hand, are special purpose-made shears for cutting overhanging grass blades away from the borders of the lawn. They feature long handles so that you do not have to bend down too far; this in my experience is better than a lawn edging tool as it does not cut chunks of soil off.

If you have a large garden with many borders, you may wish to consider using a petrol or an electric lawn edger. These are purpose-made machines for edging lawns. They look similar to small walk-behind lawnmowers but with a vertically rotating blade affixed to the front. They edge the lawn using a similar process to a lawn edging tool, cutting chunks of soil and grass off the edge of the lawn; whilst I maintain that a lawn edging tool is not very effective, I will admit that a lawn edging machine can save long hours of physical labour especially if you have a large number of borders to edge.

Lawn edging tool

Some strimmers also offer a lawn edging function, however, these are not always effective.

Roller

Rolling is an important part of lawn care, I explain this further in the 'Rolling' section of chapter six. To carry out this task you will need a lawn roller. The type of roller to use should be decided depending on the size of the lawn. There are many different types of lawn roller; from small 50 cm wide ones to large three-metre-wide models. Most rollers are supplied as

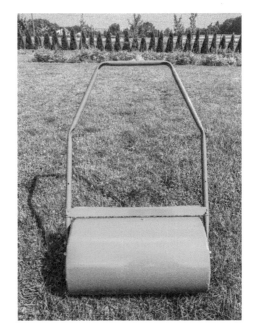

Push along lawn roller

23

empty metal cylinders and you can fill them with either water or ballast, giving them the desired weight (not all rollers are suitable to be filled with water so do check your particular one).

Tow-behind lawn roller

If your lawn is smaller than half an acre, you should be fine to use a push-along roller, this should have sufficient weight to effectively carry out the task however when filling it do bear in mind that you will have to be able to push or pull it along. Even if you are a bodybuilder, you will find that pushing or pulling a heavy roller up and down your lawn can be surprisingly exhausting.

If you have a garden that is larger than half an acre and you have a ride-on mower or other machines that are suitable for towing garden attachments; you should consider using a towable roller. A towable roller works using the same principles as a push-along one, the only differences being that a towable roller has a different shaped frame with a towing hitch on it. A push-along one has a frame with a handlebar suitable for a human to push or pull. Towable rollers are also usually wider than push-along models. There is a multitude of benefits to using one of these rollers which include the following: most towable rollers are wider than push along models (which is great because the wider the roller, the quicker you get the job done); a towable roller means that all the heavy labour is done by the machine that you are using to tow the roller (you do not have to endure the painful process of pulling a roller up a slope).

Scarifier

Scarification is also a vital part of lawncare; I explain this in the 'Scarification' Section of chapter six. As with most garden machinery there is a wide range of scarifiers to choose from. These include electric ones, petrol ones and even ride-on mower attachments. Petrol and electric scarifiers look remarkably similar to walk-behind lawnmowers and are available in push-along and self-propelled models.

If you have a garden that is smaller than a quarter of an acre, an electric scarifier should be suitable. These are available in both corded and cordless versions and just like with lawnmowers both have advantages and disadvantages. A corded electric model means that the machine is likely to be more powerful and can run for an unlimited amount of time, however you are restricted by the length of a power cable and have to take care not to damage it. A cordless machine, on the other hand, means that you are not restricted by the power cable, however the machine is likely to be less powerful and the run-time is limited by the battery. For relatively small gardens, these machines are rather reliable and effective however, using them in a garden too large can prove to be tedious. If your garden is tiny, you could also use a spring tine rake as a scarifier; vigorously pulling it through the grass.

Use a spring tine rake if you have a tiny garden

If you have a medium-sized lawn (up to 0.5 acre), it is best to use a petrol scarifier. A petrol scarifier is likely to be more powerful than an electric one and obviously you do not have to worry about a cord. Both petrol and electric scarifiers are available in self-propelled and push-along models. If your lawn is relatively level, you should be fine to use a push-along model. They are reasonably light and the horizontally rotating axel with the small blades, or tines, does help to push the machine along. If, however, you have a lawn with steep banks or slopes that you wish to scarify, you should consider using a self-propelled scarifier. This will mean that you can simply walk behind the machine, not having to push the machine up slopes. Regardless of whether they are self-propelled, these machines are extremely reliable and very powerful. As effective as these machines are, even if the machine features a collector box for the moss and thatch - you should be prepared for the inevitable task of having to rake any leftovers up off the lawn.

Petrol scarifier

Finally, if you have a lawn that is larger than half an acre and use a ride-on mower to mow it, you should consider using a ride-on mower with a rear PTO so that you can operate a powered scarifier attachment with it. This way you can make quick work of scarifying your lawn without even having to leave the driver's seat. If you are using one of these machines, once you have scarified the lawn, you can simply use a powered grass collector to collect the thatch and moss that has been ripped out by the scarifier. There is no need for the hassle of using a rake on a large lawn.

Scarifier cassette for machine with rear PTO

Dethatcher

Dethatching can be a useful part of lawn care. I explain why in the 'Dethatching' section of chapter six. Several different pieces of equipment are suitable for dethatching a lawn, from dethatching rakes to large tow-behind implements.

If you have a small to medium-sized lawn, you should be fine to use a dethatching rake; this is simply a rake with specialised blade-like tines for ripping thatch and moss out of the lawn. As far as dethatchers go this is reasonably effective. For appropriate use, you should pull it through the lawn as vigorously as possible.

Dethatching rake

If you have a garden that is half an acre or larger and a machine that is suitable for towing garden attachments, you may wish to use a towable spring-tine dethatcher. These usually consist of a large frame with a towing hitch, and multiple spring-tines designed to hook into the thatch and moss, ripping it out as the attachment moves along. These are also relatively effective; however, I maintain that a scarifier is far more effective as it does a more thorough job of removing moss and not just thatch.

Aerator

Aerating the lawn is a very useful task to carry out. I explain this process in the 'Aeration' section of chapter seven. If you decide to aerate your lawn, you will require an appropriate piece of equipment to do this. As with most garden tasks, there are a variety of different tools that can be used to carry it out.

Aerating sandal

If you have a small to medium-sized lawn, it is fine to use purpose-made aerating sandals with spikes that can be affixed to the bottom of your shoes and are supposed to aerate as you walk along the lawn. However, in my experience, many of these can often be flimsy and ineffective. If you have a relatively small lawn it is more effective to use an alternative tool, such as an aerating roller. This is a roller with a handle that looks similar to a wall painting roller but has spikes attached to it. It can be pushed along the lawn to create the holes and hence it can be quite effective. Alternatively, for deeper holes, you may wish to use a hollow-tine fork. This takes out cores of soil in each tine thus creating wide holes for air, water, and nutrients to pass through, although it is very effective, this technique can be very damaging if used more frequently than once every three years.

For small lawns, a garden fork can be used, with this you need to push the fork into the ground then pull it back and repeat this until you have covered the entire lawn. Alternatively, there are petrol push along aerators which use either hollow-tine or spiked discs to aerate – the disadvantage to these is that they are often unreasonably expensive.

Garden fork

Tow-behind aerator

Some push along scarifiers also offer an aerator function, however, if you choose to use one of these you should make sure that the machine is definitely on the aerator function, as aeration can be carried out more frequently than scarification and accidentally using a scarifier to aerate could be disastrous. Overly frequent scarification would wear out the lawn.

If you have a large lawn (0.5 acres or larger) and a machine that is suitable for towing garden attachments, you may wish to consider investing in a towable aerator that can be towed behind a ride-on mower or quad. A towable aerator uses the same principle as the aerating roller but on a larger scale. In most cases, one of these aerators has a frame with a towing hitch on it and a wide axel with either multiple spiked discs, or hollow-tine discs on it, these rotate as the attachment is pulled along to create small holes. Alternatively, some lawn rollers offer an option to affix purpose-made spikes to them, this works just as well. These attachments are very useful, as similarly to a towable roller it saves you the heavy labour and being wider, it gets the job done faster. If you are using a towable aerator it is best to avoid having to reverse your machine, as these attachments are exceptionally difficult to reverse.

Clearing leaves is an important part of maintaining the lawn in the Autumn and Winter. If your lawn is too big to be cleared of leaves using a rake, you may wish to consider using machinery such as a leaf blower or leaf vacuum to make the task that bit easier.

Some people may wish to use a leaf blower, which is a purpose-made machine that uses air to blow leaves. A leaf blower allows you to blow the leaves into a pile where you can gather them up and dispose of them. Leaf blowers come in a wide range of different models.

If you have a relatively small lawn, an electric one may be sufficient. Electric leaf blowers are usually handheld machines and are available in both corded and cordless models. Similarly, to most garden machinery

Electric corded leaf blower

Petrol handheld leaf blower

a corded electric model means more power, whereas a cordless model means that you are not limited by an electrical cord.

If your garden is larger than a quarter of an acre, using an electric leaf blower may prove ineffective, therefore, you may wish to use a petrol leaf blower. These machines are available in handheld models as well as larger backpack versions. They also come in two and four-stroke models, like petrol strimmers. Four-stroke models are known to be more reliable than two-stroke ones. Four-stroke models are also more practical as you can use the same unleaded petrol that you may use in a petrol lawnmower. Handheld models are usually lighter than backpack ones, as most of them have smaller, less powerful engines. Using a handheld leaf blower is

Petrol backpack leaf blower

suitable for areas up to half an acre. However, if your garden is larger than half an acre, using a handheld machine can be rather challenging as the operator is required to carry the machine around whilst it is being used and although these machines are relatively light they do still have a fair bit of weight. Therefore, if your garden is larger than half an acre, you may wish to use a backpack leaf blower.

Backpack machines operate by the same principles as handheld ones; however, they usually have larger, more powerful engines and consequently are capable of getting the job done quicker. Although having a larger engine means more weight; due to the backpack feature of the leaf blower's design with the carrying straps, the machine feels lighter to carry around for long periods than a handheld one. Some people are opposed to leaf blowers because you have to manually gather up the leaves after using it and windy weather conditions affect its efficiency if this is your point of view you may wish to consider using a leaf vacuum. Leaf vacuums are very similar to blowers, but they vacuum the leaves up into a collection bag or box making the disposal of the leaves easier. There are many different types of leaf vacuum; from handheld models to larger walk-behind ones, these are both available in electric and petrol models. Many handheld leaf blowers offer a vacuum function; therefore, most handheld leaf vacuums look almost identical to blowers. They have essentially the same advantages and disadvantages whether you use a corded or cordless electric model. The only real difference between handheld vacuums and walk-behind ones is that the walk-behind models save the exhaustion of having to carry the machine.

If your garden is larger than half an acre and you wish to use a leaf vacuum, a petrol walk-behind model is most suitable. These are available in push-along and self-propelled models and offer the advantages of having a large collector bag, or box, for the debris. These have more powerful engines and the advantage of not having to carry the machine. For people with extraordinarily large gardens, leaf blowers and vacuums are both available in large commercial-grade models, which can be towed behind a ride-on mower or quad. If you have a large lawn and require a ride-on mower you could also consider purchasing a ride-on mower with a powered grass collector.

This uses rotating brushes to collect the grass clippings when mowing but can also be used to collect leaves and debris without engaging the cutting deck. If you have one of these machines you do not necessarily require a leaf blower or vacuum.

Alternatively, you could consider using a mechanical lawn sweeper. These use the same principle of the rotating brushes; however, the brushes are affixed to an axle that is rotated by the turning of the wheels on the actual sweeper requiring no petrol or electricity. These lawn sweepers are available in push-along models as well as larger towable models if you are using a ride-on mower or quad. A lawn sweeper is not as effective as a powered grass collector however it still gets the job done.

Towable lawn sweeper

Spreader

If you have a medium to large-sized lawn, you are likely to need a spreader to carry out tasks such as overseeding and fertilising. If your lawn is smaller than a quarter of an acre you should be fine to use a small handheld broadcast spreader.

Handheld spreader

However, if your lawn is larger than a quarter of an acre, you may wish to use a larger, drop or broadcast spreader. These are available in both push-along and towable versions. A drop spreader usually has two wheels with a wide hopper positioned close to the ground with a metal frame that has either a handlebar or towing hitch affixed to it; the substance that you are spreading is dispensed through the bottom of the hopper. The advantage of a drop spreader is that with the hopper being close to the ground, it dispenses the same amount of the substance that you are spreading everywhere in its spreading width. So, it can be moved up and down the lawn similarly to a lawnmower and will equally cover the lawn. A disadvantage of the drop spreader is that for it to work effectively the spreader should only be moved along the lawn incredibly slowly, which means that it takes a very long time for a large lawn to be covered.

Push-along broadcast spreader

The alternative to this is a broadcast spreader. This usually consists of a slightly smaller hopper positioned high up from the ground, the substance is dispensed through the bottom of the hopper onto a horizontally rotating plate which then throws the substance onto the lawn, the plate is driven by the two wheels turning and there is usually a handlebar or towing hitch attached to the spreader. An advantage of using a broadcast spreader is that is can be moved along at a higher speed, meaning it gets the job done quicker. A disadvantage of a broadcast spreader includes the fact that it can be affected by weather conditions, causing it to be less accurate, for example: in windy conditions, the substance might be blown away by the wind before reaching the ground. For ride-on mowers that feature rear PTOs, there are also powered broadcast spreaders where the rotating plate is driven by a PTO belt and not the wheels.

No matter what spreader you opt for, you should not use the same spreader to spread fertiliser and grass seed as you would spread rock salt unless the instructions for your particular spreader state that you can. This is because whilst most spreaders are suitable for spreading substances such as fertiliser and grass seed, many spreaders are not suitable for spreading rock salt.

Additional guidance

If you are planning to purchase a large piece of garden machinery such as a petrol lawnmower irrespective of whether it is a ride-on or walk-behind model, it is likely to require annual servicing. Most manufacturers of garden machinery only offer guarantees or warranties subject to annual servicing by a licensed service centre. Therefore, if you are planning to purchase a large garden machine, you should consider whether you wish to make use of the guarantee or warranty and if so, check whether your guarantee or warranty is a conditional one. If your machine comes with a conditional guarantee or warranty, you should make sure there is a licensed service centre that offers servicing for that particular brand near your location, before purchasing the machine. It is also worth noting that in the case of lawnmowers regardless of whether they are walk-behind or ride-on models, they may require maintenance tasks such as oil changes or air filter changes to be carried out more frequently than once a year. These tasks are quite simple to do and can usually be carried out in a garden shed by someone with limited DIY skills. Omitting to carry out these tasks does not necessarily mean that your machine will immediately stop working, however, it can make the machine less reliable or even dangerous and it can also halve the machine's lifetime. It is also worth thoroughly cleaning your equipment after use, for example with a deck washout port on a lawnmower, small cleaning and maintenance tasks can be the difference between whether your equipment lasts five or ten years.

Finally, if you have a four-stroke petrol garden machine (whatever it may be) and you are planning to store petrol in a fuel can for periods longer than twenty-four hours, it is worth bearing in mind that many pieces of garden machinery have very sensitive carburettors. If unleaded petrol is stored in a petrol can for a long period of time, it is likely to 'go off'. When you put such petrol in your machine you risk causing serious damage to the carburettor. This means the machine either will not turn on or will continuously cut out seconds after being turned on. You will then have to go through the costly process of cleaning or replacing the carburettor. Therefore, it is best to add a purpose-made fuel stabiliser to the petrol on the same day as you have purchased the petrol, as this will preserve it for up to two years. Alternatively, you could decide to use a specialised alkylate petrol which does not 'go off'; this can be acquired from garden machinery shops and internet retailers.

Adding fuel stabiliser to petrol

Chapter two

Developing a lawn from scratch

Often a lawn is so damaged or worn down that there is no way of repairing it, or maybe there is not a lawn at all. If you have just moved into a new house for example there may just be a patch of flat soil in your garden. If this is the case, you need to establish a new lawn.

This should ideally be done at the beginning of spring (no later than the end of March) but it can also be done in the early autumn (preferably

end of September to start of October when there is no frost). It should be done in these seasons because there is a perfect balance of moisture in the ground and the sunlight is also just right. In the winter it is too wet with not enough sunlight and in the summer the ground is too dry. It is also worth noting that the success rate of establishing lawns in the autumn is lower than in the spring. An advantage of doing this in the spring is warmer weather, however, you may need to water the lawn more frequently. The Autumn means there is less need for watering, however, you run the risk of heavy rains washing away the grass seed.

Grass seed or turf rolls can both be used to establish a lawn; they are both available with a variety of different capabilities. You may wish to use a shade-tolerant type of turf roll due to having a lot of trees in your garden or opt for a heavy-duty grass seed due to your lawn receiving a lot of foot traffic[5]. Whichever you require, be sure to inspect your lawn and select the right type for your requirements. Most grass seed and turf rolls can be purchased from garden centres as well as from internet suppliers.

In my experience the best way of establishing a lawn is by using turf rolls, this is faster and will give you a thicker and more consistent lawn than grass seed. Regardless of the size of the area of the garden in which you intend to establish the lawn, or whether you are using turf rolls or grass seed, the following steps must be taken.

Preparation

The site for the new lawn must be adequately prepared. Most sites for new lawns are already covered with weeds and some grass. If this is the case, you should first treat the site with weed killer, this will stop existing weeds from coming through when the new lawn is in place. Once there are no weeds on the site, it is worth loosening the soil, if you have a small garden this can be done by digging it over, using a spade or fork, and if you have a large garden you may wish to use a rotavator. Once the soil has been loosened you should take the opportunity to use your feet and/or a hoe to break up any large chunks of soil and flatten the site as it should be as smooth as possible with no bumps or holes in it. Whilst you are doing this, any debris such as roots, rocks, or leftover weeds should be removed; if your lawn needs to be levelled, this is when it should be done. During this time, you should also be able to see how much topsoil there is on the site and how good the quality of it is. You should only have topsoil near the surface therefore if the layer of topsoil on the surface of the site is less than three to six inches thick,

you should order more. If your garden is made up of clay or chalk dominated soil, you should cover the site with three to six inches[6] of topsoil as this will vastly improve the soil quality. You do not have to order more topsoil if the layer is already six inches thick. Be sensible and bear in mind that if your garden is on a slope, you have just applied six inches of topsoil, and it is not adequately compacted – heavy rainfall could cause mini landslides in your garden.

Topsoil can be spread out using a landscape rake, or if you have a large garden you can use a ladder to spread it by laying the ladder flat on the ground, tying a rope to it and using the rope to pull the ladder along. After applying topsoil, the newly smoothed site should be lightly compacted, using your feet if you have a small site and a light lawn roller if you have a large one. Once the topsoil on the site is smooth, you should apply a thin layer of sharp sand (no more than two inches thick) on top of your topsoil, this is not a necessary step, but it can help to improve the quality of the topsoil. A landscape rake or a ladder can be used to smooth out the sand. The sand and topsoil can both be purchased in large quantities from builder's merchants as well as certain garden centres and internet retailers.

Turf rolls

Once the area has been prepared, it is time to apply the turf rolls. These should be applied as soon as possible, ideally within 48 hours of you acquiring them, so they do not dry out. Most turf rolls measure 1ft by 3ft7 and are rolled up like rugs when sold. To apply the turf rolls you should unroll them and neatly place them on the ground where you wish to lay them (obviously with the grass side facing upwards). It is best to ensure that the turf rolls are laid as close to each other as possible without gaps between them or them overlapping. Scissors or a Stanley knife can be used to cut the turf rolls to the shape and size you want them; it is similar to laying tiles. Once the turf rolls have been laid out and cut to size you should fill any gaps with leftover topsoil or sand and a bit of grass seed.

Immediately after laying the turf rolls, you should water them generously If it is not raining. The new lawn should be generously watered once a day for four weeks after it has been laid, this will ensure that the turves can develop adequate roots. If the turves are not regularly watered in this vital four-week period, it can lead to them drying out and mean having to lay new ones. Once the four weeks have passed you no longer need to water the lawn every day, however, if it is particularly dry the lawn should still be watered generously. It is also useful, but not absolutely necessary to roll the new lawn with a light roller a few days after the turves have been laid, this will help the roots penetrate the ground and compact the turves.

In the four-week period after your turf rolls have been laid, the lawn is just settling in, therefore, as well as regularly watering your lawn it is best to limit foot traffic to only when necessary such as when you are watering your lawn. After the four-week period your lawn is ready for the first cut.

Grass seed

Once the site has been prepared, it is time to apply the grass seed. This should be done in dry weather, preferably not in windy conditions. It is best to ensure that the grass seed is evenly spread; bear in mind that not all of the seeds you sow are going to develop into grass blades. You should be generous with how much seed you use and spread the seeds thicker than you would think is reasonable. If you have a relatively small garden, you can simply spread the seed in handfuls or use a small handheld broadcast spreader. However, if your garden is larger than a quarter of an acre, you should consider using a larger drop spreader or broadcast spreader, these are both available in push along models as well as ones that can be towed behind a ride-on mower or quad depending on your requirements.

Once the grass seed has been spread, it is best to spread a very thin (approximately one inch thick) layer of topsoil (fine compost also works) on top of the grass seed; the topsoil should be spread evenly so you may wish to use a landscape rake to do this. Spreading the topsoil

will provide the grass seed with somewhere to develop its fine roots at an early stage of development, it will help to store water, it will also discourage birds from eating the grass seed.

When the topsoil has been spread, whilst some people do not support this method, in my experience, it is useful to lightly compact the topsoil with the grass seed. If your lawn is relatively small you can do this by putting down a plywood board, standing on it, then moving it over and repeating the process. However, if your lawn is a quarter of an acre or larger you should use a lawn roller, a lawn roller is a worthwhile investment as you will need it for the annual task of rolling.

Once you have compacted your topsoil and grass seed, you should wait for three to four days for the seeds to settle, then if it is not

raining, proceed to water it. If it does not rain, you should generously water your grass seed once a day for four weeks after it has been spread, this will ensure that the grass seed can develop adequate roots. When watering, take great care not to wash the seeds out of place, it helps to use a fine spray head on a hose-pipe nozzle. Once the four weeks have passed, you no longer need to water your lawn every day, however, if it is particularly dry you should still water it generously.

During the four-week period, you should start to see the grass seed developing into small grass blades. These blades need time to strengthen and become thicker before they can be walked on, or mowed, therefore as well as regularly watering your lawn, you should also limit foot traffic to when absolutely necessary. After a four to eight-week period your lawn might be ready for the first cut. You should judge this based on how long and how thick the grass blades are; mowing premature grass blades could be disastrous. Simply pushing the lawnmower over weak grass blades could tear them out.

Chapter three

Refurbishing an existing lawn

Many lawns fall into a state of neglect, if you are not much of a lawncare enthusiast, or you just haven't had the time to tend to your lawn the way you should have done, the lawn may have started to deteriorate. Refurbishment is required when you need to do something about the lawn, but it is not quite bad enough to replace.

Refurbishment is a very intensive project for the lawn and should only be carried out if necessary. It is like renovating a house, if it is carried out incorrectly, refurbishing a lawn can do more harm than good, it might weaken and damage a good lawn.

Therefore, you should always assess whether your lawn requires to be refurbished based on whether it shows the majority of the following characteristics:

- An abnormally large number of weeds (more weeds than grass)
- An abnormally large build-up of moss and/or thatch (more moss than grass)
- Many and/or large bare or brown patches
- Weak and/or unhealthy grass

Different gardeners swear by different methods, in my experience, the following method is the most effective.

Refurbishment of an existing lawn should be carried out in the spring, as it is rather a long process that requires a great amount of moisture and also sufficient sunlight (the autumn period is not long enough). Refurbishing a lawn is essentially a period of intensive versions of general maintenance being carried out.

Assuming that the lawn contains large amounts of moss and thatch, the first step of the project is to thoroughly scarify the lawn. This will remove any undesirable thatch and moss, meaning that the grass receives more sunlight, has access to more nutrients and has more space to grow. You should mow whatever is left of the previous lawn on the lowest possible setting before scarifying (never mow the lawn on the lowest setting unless you are refurbishing it).

Next, you should treat the lawn with a type of lawn fertiliser that 'feeds and weeds' (ensure that this takes place in one of the suitable months indicated for the specific fertiliser that you are using). I would not recommend this type of fertiliser for any use other than lawn refurbishment. This is because it literally kills off anything in your lawn other than grass, therefore when this fertiliser is applied it turns approximately 80% of most domestic lawns into black spots of dead weeds. In this particular case, this is not a problem, as you will have to re-seed the lawn later anyway.

Once the feed and weed fertiliser has killed off all the undesirable weeds in your lawn, you should use a spring-tine rake to remove the dried-up black weeds from it. This will free up space for you to sow new seeds.

At this point, if there is any debris or any undesirable objects on the lawn such as rocks or tree stumps, you should remove them. Tree roots or stumps especially need to be removed as they may sprout up through the lawn at a later stage.

Next, you should use either a purpose-made top dressing or a mixture of topsoil and sand to fill in any holes or uneven space in the lawn. It is best to use a landscape rake or a ladder with a rope to spread the mixture or top dressing to be smooth and to make sure that it fills-in any holes and levels the ground, it also helps to use a lawn roller to compact this top dressing or mixture if you have one available.

Once the ground and what is left of the previous lawn has been flattened, you should spread grass seed on any bare patches as well as on top of existing grass to make it thicker. You should overseed using the method for sowing grass seed described in the Grass seed section of chapter two.

When the grass seed has been spread and it is covered with a thin layer of topsoil or fine compost, you should water your lawn once a day for four weeks as explained in chapter

one and limit foot traffic on the newly refurbished lawn. As time passes maintenance tasks such as mowing and applying a general fertiliser (not feed and weed) should continue to be done at the appropriate intervals. You should not scarify the lawn for a minimum of two years after it has been refurbished. This is because the scarification combined with the feed and weed fertiliser during the refurbishment would have done such a thorough job of removing any moss or thatch that is very unlikely that it should come back in less than two years. Scarifying a lawn that does not have thatch or moss in it is an absurd idea, as it will just tear out the perfectly good grass blades and unnecessarily weaken the lawn as a whole.

Chapter four

Weekly tasks

The tasks I will be explaining in this chapter should be carried out on a weekly to two-weekly basis in the growing season, which, in Great Britain takes place between March and November. This is because these tasks are related to the speed at which the grass is growing; they

are the ones that require to be carried out most frequently out of all the lawn maintenance tasks in this book.

Apart from watering, these tasks do not require to be done any more frequently than once a week or outside the growing season. Carrying out these tasks more frequently than this, or outside the growing season, could be damaging to the lawn.

I have not put the tasks in any particular order, as they do not rely on each other to be carried out.

The tasks I will be explaining in this chapter should be carried out on a weekly to two weekly basis in the growing season, which, in Great Britain takes place between March and November. This is because these tasks are related to the speed at which the grass is growing; they are the ones that require to be carried out most frequently out of all the lawn maintenance tasks in this book. Apart from watering, these tasks do not require to be done any more frequently than once a week or outside the growing season. Carrying out these tasks more frequently than this, or outside the growing season, could be damaging to the lawn. I have not put the tasks in any particular order, as they do not rely on each other to be carried out.

Lawnmowing

The first very obvious task is lawn mowing, which should be done once every week in the growing season. For commercial lawns such as cricket pitches, you might need to mow more frequently, however, mowing once a week is sufficient for most domestic lawns. Common sense should still be used to judge the frequency, for example, if it is very dry and the grass has not grown much, it is fine to mow after two weeks. The first cut of the year should be done in March depending on weather conditions; for mowing the lawn the weather should be relatively dry. If moist grass is clogging up your lawnmower it means you are doing something wrong. You should especially not mow your lawn in wet conditions if you have a ride-on mower, as there is likely to be wheelspin that will tear your lawn apart. The first cut of the year (in March) should be done using a higher lawnmower setting than usual; for example, if you normally use number three, the first cut should be done in number four or even five. This is because the lawn will be particularly weak after having been in what is essentially hibernation for the winter. Therefore, cutting at a higher setting allows the lawn to grow accustomed to being mowed again. Then after the lawn has recovered from the first cut, the second cut can be carried out at the usual height.

You should decide what length you wish to have your lawn; the average length of a healthy lawn is between two and three inches after being mowed. However, this can vary depending on how bumpy or otherwise the lawn is and what type of grass it is made up of (you do not want to have grass that is too short). It is worth inspecting the height of the grass blades in your lawn before mowing. You need to ensure that whatever height you select, you do not cut more than approximately one-third of the grass blades off at one time. Cutting off more than one-third of the grass blades in one go can be very damaging to the lawn. It can shock what's left of the grass making it turn a light brown colour, weakening it and making it easier for weeds and moss to inhabit the area; it can also cause scalping. Most lawnmowers will have height settings in numbers on them, it is worth noting that the numbers on a lawnmower do not necessarily stand for units of measurements such as inches. The heights for each number can also vary depending on the make and model of the lawnmower, for example, number three on one brand of lawnmower might be a different height to number three on a different brand of mower.

To successfully mow a lawn, you will need at least two pieces of equipment these are: a lawnmower and a strimmer. The lawnmower will give the main part of the lawn a nice neat cut and the strimmer is needed to cut the grass blades near the edges of the lawn, such as, next to fences where most lawnmowers would not fit. Strimming the edges of your lawn will provide it with a nice, clean frame. Just like most pieces of garden equipment lawnmowers and strimmers both come in a wide range of different sizes with different capabilities, if you have a relatively small lawn an electric lawnmower and strimmer may be suitable for you. However, if your lawn is larger than a quarter of an acre you may wish to use a petrol lawnmower and strimmer; these are likely to be larger and more powerful. If your lawn is particularly large (0.5 acres or larger) you may wish to invest in a ride-on mower and a large petrol strimmer as these will enable you to mow your lawn faster. The most common type of domestic lawnmower is a rotary one, this is because the alternative (a cylinder mower) is only really worthwhile if your lawn is the quality of a cricket pitch.

There is also a range of different ways to deal with the grass clippings that are left after having mowed your lawn; some people use a grass collector to pick up their grass clippings and others prefer mulching. You should ensure that you choose the right option for you and your lawn. I explain this topic at more depth in the 'Dealing with grass clipping' section of chapter seven.

Regardless of what lawnmower you are using, you should mow the entire lawn on the same height setting and preferably on the same day to achieve an even finish. Before mowing, you should also make sure that there is no debris such as twigs or rocks on the lawn, as these could damage the lawnmower blades. To mow correctly you should push or drive (as appropriate) the lawnmower up and down parallel with the longest side of the lawn in overlapping strips to ensure that you do not miss any grass blades, which would look very dissatisfying later (I personally find grass blades which stick up in the middle of the lawn, after it having been mowed, incredibly irritating). When the main part of the lawn has been mowed you should push or drive the lawnmower around the edge of your lawn to frame it in neatly. Finally, after the lawn has been mowed, the strimmer should be used to strim the grass at the edges of the lawn.

Weeding

Weeding your lawn is a task that should be done approximately once a week in the growing season; however, it is not as crucial to do it every week as, for example, mowing is. It is only really worth bothering to remove particularly prominent or invasive weeds; these are the ones that cause bare patches when they dry out, as the lawn is green you are unlikely to see the more discrete ones. If your lawn was established using turf rolls or recently refurbished, you are unlikely to have very many weeds anyway.

The most problematic weeds in a lawn include daisies and dandelions; they should be removed at all cost. There are various ways to remove these weeds, some would recommend a feed and weed fertiliser, however, as I have mentioned it is not beneficial to use this unless you are refurbishing your lawn, or, it is already of outstanding quality (a cricket pitch). My preferred method is to pull the weeds out individually,

there are purpose-made pieces of equipment for pulling out individual weeds, these include a 'daisy grabber' and a 'weed puller'. This is, in my experience, the most effective method to use. Although I have found that you do not necessarily need to use purpose-made equipment, you can also just pull some weeds out by hand or use and old screwdriver to prize them out. I knew someone who frequently used to walk around their lawn and spent lengthy periods individually prizing weeds out.

Weeding your lawn is not affected by weather conditions or how frequently it is done although if the ground is slightly moist it makes pulling the weeds out easier.

Watering

As humorous as it may sound, even a British lawn needs to be watered. The aim of this is to ensure that your lawn stays thick and green no matter what the weather. Although I have put it in the 'weekly tasks' chapter of the book, this task requires to be carried out roughly once a day, every day in the height of the growing season; although it is fine to water only once or twice a week if it is not particularly warm. You should apply common sense and realise that if it is raining or the

ground is already sufficiently moist there is no need to water. Watering should ideally take place between April and September when the soil is dry (if you have clay soil this will affect you more), as that is when the lawn is likely to be in need of water. If it is a dry summer and the lawn does not get watered it is likely to dry out and turn a light brown colour, in the autumn, much of it will recover. However, there will inevitably be some permanent brown bare patches, which encourage the growth of weeds, and moss. You should also water once a day if you have recently laid turf rolls or sowed grass seed, as they will need extra water to help with developing initial roots. If the lawn is wet or it is not the growing season, there is absolutely no need for watering. If you do water, it is likely to do more harm than good, for example, it is likely to make the lawn waterlogged, turn parts of your lawn brown and contribute to the development of moss.

Regardless of how frequently you do it, the lawn should always be watered in the early morning (before 9 am, the earlier the better). Watering during the day is a pointless activity, as that is when the temperature is at its hottest and most of the water will evaporate before the soil absorbs it. Watering in the evening or afternoon is harmful because if the lawn is moist at night it increases the risk of diseases, moss and weeds. Watering in the early morning means that the water is absorbed before the temperature increases and helps to keep the lawn cool during the day.

There are many ways to water: if you have a tiny lawn a watering can should do the trick, for relatively small lawns using a

hose-pipe with a standard nozzle to water or an oscillating, rotary, or pulse-jet sprinkler attachment could be suitable. However, if your lawn is larger than a quarter of an acre it is worth investing in a watering system or travelling sprinkler. Most watering systems are a structure of small water pipes with multiple strategically placed rotary sprinklers,

the pipes are usually buried approximately six inches underneath the lawn, the system would be connected either to your mains water supply or an alternative water source such as a well (if you have one). Most watering systems can be programmed to water at specific times of day on certain or all days, it can also be turned off if, for example, it is raining. Some watering systems can be purchased as self-build kits, however, you could also get one professionally installed.

I whole-heartedly recommend investing in a watering system, for anyone at all, regardless of whether you have a small, medium, or large lawn. The advantages include the fact that multiple rotary sprinklers can water the lawn faster than a hose-pipe nozzle or a single sprinkler that is attached to a  hose-pipe. Another advantage is that with being able to programme the watering system, you do not even have to be at home, let alone in your garden, for your lawn to be watered. If you do opt for a watering system, walking on the lawn whilst it is in operation is not particularly harmful to the lawn, however, you are likely to get wet!

As useful as watering systems are, they are costly to install and can often require maintenance tasks to be done such as cleaning clogged up sprinklers. Therefore, an alternative solution to a watering system is a travelling sprinkler. The idea is that you lay a hose-pipe on your lawn like tracks for a model railway, where you want the sprinkler to go, then bend the end of the hose-pipe back and attach it to the travelling sprinkler. The travelling sprinkler is a three-wheeled device with a rotary sprinkler. It is propelled by the water flowing through it and follows the hosepipe around the garden whilst spraying water on the lawn. Advantages of a travelling sprinkler include that it is more affordable than a watering system and that it moves on its own, thus saving you the hassle of moving a single sprinkler around the garden. Disadvantages include that it relies on high water pressure to work effectively and that the hose-pipe has to be laid out every time before use.

Chapter five

Monthly tasks

The tasks I will be looking at in this chapter require to be carried out every month in the growing season which, in Great Britain is between March and November. This is because they are related to the speed

at which the grass is growing, and they require to be done more frequently than once a year. However, they do not require to be done every week or outside the growing season. Carrying out these tasks more frequently than once a month, or outside the growing season, could be damaging to the lawn.

I have not put the tasks in any particular order, as they do not rely on each other to be carried out.

Fertilisation

Fertilisation is the process of spreading purpose-made fertiliser on the lawn. This provides the lawn with additional nutrients that cause the lawn to be healthier, greener, and thicker. Fertilisation should generally be carried out once a month in the growing season between March and November, but make sure that you check the instructions on the specific fertiliser that you are using. Appropriate months for use and intervals between uses can vary depending on the brand or type of fertiliser you use. There is no need to fertilise before overseeding. There is a wide range of different fertilisers to serve different purposes; these can be purchased from many garden centres, hardware shops and internet retailers.

A well-known type of fertiliser is one that 'feeds and weeds', this fertiliser is designed to kill off undesirable weeds from your lawn and deliver nutrients to the grass. I would not recommend ever using this type of fertiliser unless you are using it as part of a lawn refurbishment. This is because, judging by my experiences with feed and weed, it tends to kill off most of the lawn. Unless you have very recently installed your lawn using turf rolls, your lawn is likely to have a substantial number of discrete green weeds and moss that you do not even know about. When feed and weed is applied it kills off all weeds and moss, including the discrete ones, leaving your lawn with approximately 80% of dried up weeds and moss which the fertiliser has turned black. You then have the tedious task of having to rake out the black weeds and moss, then having to re-seed the lawn, which you do not want unless you are refurbishing a lawn.

I, therefore, recommend using a type of fertiliser that just feeds; this will deliver nutrients to your lawn without killing off any weeds or moss. Most of the moss will have been ripped out earlier in the year when the lawn was scarified and the prominent weeds can be removed in other ways. This way you have a healthy green lawn without having to deal with irritating black spots. Some fertilisers also contain grass seed to

make the lawn thicker, this is a useful feature, but should not be used to replace the process of overseeding.

Regardless of what type of fertiliser you may be using, you should take the following steps to ensure that you apply it correctly: the fertiliser should be spread around your lawn evenly, the instructions for the fertiliser you are using should indicate the area that it is sufficient for, so make sure that you have purchased enough for the size of your lawn. Unless otherwise indicated for the one that you are using, it is best to spread the fertiliser using a handheld spreader if you have a small lawn and using a push-along, or towable, broadcast or drop spreader if you have a large lawn. Many fertilisers contain chemicals so make sure you take appropriate safety precautions such as wearing gloves when handling the fertiliser. It is fine to use the same spreader to fertilise as the one that you used to spread grass seed.

Once the fertiliser has been spread, most types require water to dissolve into the ground and start working, therefore if it is not raining, you can speed up the fertiliser by watering the lawn.

It is worth noting that if the lawn is overdosed with fertiliser it can act as a weed killer, causing the grass to turn brown and dry out. It is, therefore, best to use a spreader and not handfuls for fertiliser spreading and ensure that you only apply the recommended amount.

Lack of watering and/or heavy foot traffic generally does not affect the working of fertiliser, however, as a safety precaution, if there are small children or animals around you should discourage them from going near the lawn for a couple of days after having applied the fertiliser.

Lawn Edging

Lawn edging is the process of cutting back the grass from the edges of the lawn, for example where the lawn borders paths or flowerbeds, these sharp edges will give your lawn a neatly manicured look. This task should be carried out every month in the growing season, as this is when the lawn is likely to grow onto paths and other borders; there is no need to do it in the winter as the edges from the autumn should last until the spring.

Lawn edging can be carried out using a variety of different tools these include a lawn edging tool, a simple tool that looks similar to a spade; long-handled lawn edging shears, purpose-made shears for cutting the edge of the grass and a petrol or electric lawn edger, a purpose-made machine for lawn edging. Some strimmers also have a lawn edging function although, in my experience, a purpose-made tool

works considerably better. A lawn edging tool or shears are ideal if you have a relatively small lawn or not many borders, however, if you have a large lawn (larger than 0.5 acres) you should consider hiring or investing in a lawn edging machine, as this will make the task significantly faster to do.

Irrespective of what tool you are using, it is best to carry out this task in dry weather when the soil is dry but not rock solid. The tool you use (whatever it may be) will cut small chunks of grass and soil off the edge of the lawn, so make sure that you have somewhere to deposit these, a compost heap works well. It is best to ensure that if you are using a machine, you cut as little soil away as possible.

Foot traffic and watering have no effect on the edge of the lawn and it can be used as normal straight after edging is completed.

LAWN AERATION

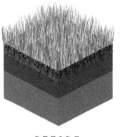

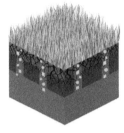

BEFORE   PROCESS   AFTER

Aeration

Aeration is the process of using a purpose-made piece of equipment to pierce small holes in the ground, a useful part of lawn care. Regardless of what type of aerator you may be using, the fundamental purpose of an aerator is to have small blades or spikes which pierce holes in the lawn, thus tackling compaction that may cause brown or bare patches. It also penetrates the build-up of moss and/or thatch, allowing the grass to have easier access to nutrients, oxygen and water.

Aeration should only be carried out in the growing season (it is particularly effective in the spring), aerating in the winter is completely pointless as the lawn is likely to be wet and soggy, meaning that you would just create mud. In the growing season, aeration can be carried out anywhere between once every two weeks to annually (do not use a hollow-tine fork more frequently than once every three years).

Aeration does not affect and is not affected by any other maintenance tasks, therefore, aerating a couple of months after scarification can be useful, as some of the moss might have come back. It would be a pointless endeavour to aerate any more frequently than once every two weeks, as the holes from the last aeration would still be present.

You also should not aerate at a time when you are minimising foot traffic, such as just after a lawn being overseeded.

There are many different types and sizes of aerator; for small and medium lawns you could use purpose-made aerating sandals with spikes that can be affixed to the bottom of your shoes, an aerating roller, or a hollow-tine fork. Some scarifiers also offer an aerating function, however, these are not always effective. For small lawns, a garden fork also works, with this you need to push the fork into the ground then pull it back and repeat the process until the entire lawn has been aerated. If you have a large lawn (0.5 acres or larger) you may wish to use an aerator that can be towed behind a ride-on mower.

Irrespective of what type of aerator you may be using, it is best to ensure that there is sufficient weight upon the aerator, if you are using a small aerating roller (depending on what the instructions state) you may need to push it down with your foot, or if you are using a towable roller you may need to affix a weight, such as concrete blocks, on top of it. This weight is necessary for the spikes to be able to push into the ground and penetrate the layers of thatch and/or moss.

Similarly, to mowing or scarifying, it is best to move the aerator up and down the lawn in overlapping strips, parallel with the longest side of the lawn, to ensure that the holes are evenly distributed and that all of the lawn has been covered.

Chapter six

Annual tasks

The tasks I will be exploring in this chapter require to be done annually (in the spring), this is because most of them are either very intensive for the lawn or they require very specific weather conditions to be carried out successfully. I have put the tasks in the order in which they should ideally be carried out. This is because many of the tasks require others to have already been completed for them to be successful. As they are annual tasks, they should not be carried out more frequently than once a year.

Rolling

The first task of the year is rolling; this consists of pushing, pulling, or towing (as appropriate) a lawn roller up and down the lawn, to compact the soil that the lawn is sitting on, after the moist conditions of the previous winter. Some experts believe that rolling can be damaging to the lawn, I agree that it should certainly not be used in an attempt to flatten the uneven ground. However, using it correctly can benefit the lawn. Rolling should be carried out in the early spring (beginning to middle of March) it should be done in the spring because that is when the ground is just wet enough to allow the roller to form it. In the summer the ground can dry out and rolling is pointless as it will not be able to compact solid dry soil; rolling in the winter can be damaging to the lawn as the ground is likely to be very wet and soggy. Lawn rolling should only be carried out after the first cut of the year. You should especially not roll in wet or winter conditions if you are towing your roller with a machine such as a ride-on mower, as there is likely to be wheel-spin which will literally tear your lawn apart. Unless you have put down grass seed and or top dressing, you should not roll more than once a year, doing so may over compact and damage the lawn.

Lawn rolling should be carried out using a purpose-made lawn roller; this is a worthwhile investment as you will need to roll your lawn annually. You may also need to use a lawn roller after applying top dressing, seeding, or refurbishing a lawn (the roller should be lighter than usual). Lawn rollers are available with a range of capabilities; you may have a small lawn and need to use a small push-along roller or have a large garden (0.5 acres or larger) and opt for a towable roller that can be towed behind a ride-on mower or quad. You should by no means ever use a whacker plate or other inappropriate piece of equipment to carry out tasks such as rolling. To successfully roll your lawn your roller should have the heaviest possible weight. You should then push or pull (tow if it is a large one) the roller up and down the lawn parallel with the longest side. Similarly to using a lawnmower, you should make sure that as you move the roller up and down, you overlap with the strip that you have just done, this way you ensure that you do not miss parts of your lawn.

Scarification

Scarification consists of pushing, pulling, or towing (as appropriate) a scarifier up and down your lawn. Scarification aims to rip out the build-up of moss and thatch that the lawn will have acquired over a wet winter. It will provide the grass with more space, nutrients and sunlight. It is best to scarify your lawn in April (before top dressing) once the ground is relatively dry and at least three weeks after the first cut of the year. Both scarification and the first cut of the year weaken the lawn; it is good to give the lawn three weeks of recovery time after the first cut before scarifying. Scarifying in April means the lawn has plenty of time to recover. You should not scarify more frequently than once a year, as this can damage the lawn. A motorised scarifier will either have multiple small blades or spring-tines attached to a horizontally rotating axel underneath it, these hook into the moss and/or thatch and rip it out of the lawn. Many people confuse the processes of scarifying, aerating, and dethatching, however, there are multiple differences so make sure that you understand the correct definition for each.

Scarifiers can come in a range of different sizes and capabilities: if you have a tiny garden a spring-tine rake works, for relatively small gardens you may need a smaller electric scarifier and if you have a larger garden you may need a larger petrol one. Some scarifiers can be attached to certain brands of walk-behind or ride-on mowers. Some machinery

hire companies also rent out scarifiers, however, it is a worthwhile investment to buy one outright as you will need to use it annually as well as to refurbish a lawn.

To successfully scarify a lawn, you should first mow the lawn at a lower setting than usual, as this will enable the scarifier to reach more of the moss. The scarifier should be used similarly to a lawnmower moving it up and down the lawn in overlapping strips, parallel with the longest side of the lawn. If the lawn has a particularly large amount of moss or thatch in it, you may also wish to scarify by moving the machine up and down parallel with the shorter side of the lawn (this will ensure that you remove as much thatch and/or moss as possible). It is worth noting that the peaty moss and thatch ripped out by the scarifier will either be collected in a collector on the machine or deposited on the lawn. If it is deposited on the lawn it should be raked up and disposed of as soon as possible. If it is left on the lawn the moss will make its way into the soil and you are back to square one. A suitable place to deposit the thatch and moss is a compost heap.

If you are planning to apply top dressing and/or grass seed (you should be) this should be done within four days of scarifying. If you leave it for too long the grass will become tall and you will have to mow it again before applying the top dressing and/or grass seed. Regardless of whether you are planning to apply top dressing and/or grass seed, you should not mow your lawn for two to three weeks after scarification because, similarly to the first cut of the year, the lawn will need time to recover. You should also minimize foot traffic during this time.

Dethatching

Many people confuse dethatching a lawn with scarifying; this is because the two are very similar. Similarly to a scarifier, a dethatcher works by making small blades or spring-tines hook into the thatch and rip it out of the lawn. The aim of dethatching is to rip out the build-up of thatch from the lawn, thus giving the grass access to more water and nutrients. It is not necessary to carry out this task and if you have, or intend to, scarify your lawn, it is completely pointless to use a dethatcher as it is simply a less effective version of a scarifier. Whilst it rips out the thatch, it is considerably less effective at removing moss than a scarifier. If you do choose to use a dethatcher, it is best to carry out this process at the same time of year as you would scarify (in April) as it is a similarly intensive process for the lawn.

Multiple different pieces of equipment can be used for dethatching. If you have a small to a medium-sized garden, you could use a dethatching rake and if you have a garden that is larger than half an acre you may wish to use a towable spring-tine dethatcher.

Similarly, to mowing and scarification, dethatching should be carried out by moving the dethatcher up and down the lawn in overlapping stripes, parallel with the longest side. This will ensure that you have not missed out any spots. Dethatchers usually do not completely remove the thatch from the lawn; they simply pull it so that the thatch is no longer lying flat on the ground but sticking up like abnormally long grass blades. Therefore, to remove the thatch from the lawn completely, it is beneficial to mow over the freshly dethatched lawn with a collecting lawnmower, as this will remove and collect the strands of thatch.

Just like scarification, if you intend to apply top dressing and/or grass seed, this should be done within four days of dethatching. This is because if you leave the grass to grow for too long, it will become tall and you will have to mow it again before applying the top dressing and/or grass seed. The lawn can be mowed immediately after dethatching as it is slightly less overwhelming than scarification. Although dethatching is a perfectly reasonable means to remove thatch and moss from the lawn, I maintain that in my experience, it is not as effective as scarification.

Top dressing

Top dressing is the process of spreading topsoil, sand, or a purpose-made top dressing (a mixture of sand and soil) on top of your lawn. The aim of top dressing is to even out the bumps and holes in the lawn as well as to improve the quality of the topsoil. Improving the quality of the topsoil will encourage the growth of both the existing grass and newly planted grass seed. Some believe that this job should be carried out in the autumn, which has its advantages, however, in my experience top dressing should be done in April just after the beginning of the mowing season, as this is the time when the lawn will recover the fastest.

There is a wide range of different types of top dressing to choose from: there is sand, a mixture of sand and topsoil and other purpose-made top dressings. These are all available from most garden centres, builder's merchants, and internet retailers. In places with good quality topsoil, many people choose to simply use sand as a top dressing, that is fine, grass generally reacts well to sand in places where the topsoil is of good quality already. However, in places with poor quality soil such as clay, using sand as top dressing can be disastrous, as depending on weather conditions it will either just run off the clay or mix with it and become an even harder concrete-like mixture. Therefore, if the soil in your garden is made up of predominantly clay, you should either use topsoil or

a purpose-made top dressing, this will improve the quality of your topsoil by helping to break up the clay.

To successfully carry out the task of top dressing, you should spread an even layer of your chosen top dressing on your lawn. The layer should be no more than one or two inches thick (you will build it up over time) it is not the end of the world if the layer is slightly thicker, you should use a landscape rake or a ladder with a rope to spread the top dressing, if your lawn is particularly large you may also wish to hire or invest in a piece of specialised equipment such as those used on golf courses to spread top dressing. Spreading this even one or two-inch-thick layer will ensure that the grass blades are still able to grow through it, and over time it will improve the quality of the topsoil in your garden.

Do not be surprised if immediately after applying the top dressing your lawn looks worse than it did before because the top dressing will be sitting on top of the grass blades. This will soon change; as the grass grows the grass blades will grow through the topdressing eventually making the top dressing disappear. If you regularly water the lawn the top dressing will disappear sooner, if you mow the lawn just before top dressing (or top dress within four days after scarifying) there is less grass blade for the substance to sit on top of. If you are planning to apply grass seed (overseeding) you should do so within four days of having applied the top dressing, otherwise, you will need to use even more topsoil when you apply the grass seed.

Overseeding

Overseeding is the process of spreading grass seed over an existing lawn. This task aims to make the lawn thicker, fill-in any bare patches and fill-in space previously occupied by thatch and/or moss with grass. This should take place in the spring, ideally within four days after having applied the top dressing.

It is best to have slightly loose topsoil before spreading the grass seed; if you are carrying out this task within four days (you should be) of having applied the top dressing it is fine. If more than four days have passed, or you haven't applied any top dressing, it is best to spread a very thin layer (approximately one inch thick) of topsoil or sand on top of the existing lawn in the area you wish to seed. Having a thin layer of loose topsoil, top dressing, or sand means that the newly sowed grass seed will have somewhere to easily develop its early roots.

Once the loose material (topsoil etc.) has been applied, the next step is to spread the grass seed evenly over the existing grass as well as on any brown patches or bare patches. The grass seed should be spread with a very thick consistency, not all of the grass seed is going to grow and you will also lose a considerable amount to birds, so spread more than what common sense would tell you to.

If you have a relatively small lawn it works fine to spread the grass seed using your hands or a small handheld broadcast spreader.

However, if you have a lawn that is larger than a quarter of an acre, I recommend that you consider investing in a larger broadcast, or drop spreader, as it will make your life much easier. A spreader is a worthwhile investment as, similarly to the roller and scarifier, you will need it at least once a year; it can also be used to spread fertiliser.

Immediately after the grass seed has been spread, it is useful to spread a very thin layer of topsoil or fine compost, on top of it using

a landscape rake. This layer will provide the newly sowed grass seed with protection from birds as well as further space to develop roots. After having spread the final layer of topsoil, it is beneficial to compact the newly sowed seed and the topsoil together using a lawn roller.

As I have mentioned in the Grass Seed section of chapter two, after spreading and compacting the final layer of topsoil, if it has not rained a few days after the task was carried out, the area of lawn with the newly sowed seeds should be generously watered (you do need to take care not to wash out the grass seed). Watering should be continued once a day for four weeks (if there is no rain) after overseeding has been carried out. As I have mentioned, after the four-week period you no longer need to water your lawn daily, however, you should still water if the weather is particularly dry.

The lawn should not be mowed for two to three weeks after overseeding has been carried out. Foot traffic should also be minimized at this time.

Chapter seven

Handy tips

In this chapter, I will explain some useful tips and methods for carrying out garden tasks that I have found invaluable over the years.

Adequate length

Your lawn must be cut at the right length. The right length is when the grass blades in the lawn are consistently at the same length. As discussed in the 'lawn mowing' section of chapter three, you should only be cutting one-third of the grass blade each time. Mowing the lawn, at too low a setting can cause scalping and bare patches. Similarly, if the lawn is mowed more frequently than once a week, it would result in too much of the grass blade being removed and the grass being shocked.

If the lawn is mowed infrequently or has not been mowed for longer than two weeks in the growing season, it is worth ensuring that you are still only cutting one-third of the grass blade off at a time. If for example, the lawn is abnormally long, it is best to mow it at a higher setting than usual and gradually reduce the height at each cut. Do not forget you should still wait at least one week between cuts.

Adequate thickness and consistency

A key element of a successful lawn is to have thick grass blades consistently throughout. Thicker grass will make the lawn look neater, reduce the availability of space for weeds, and help with the visibility of stripes.

Several factors contribute to having a thick lawn. One of these factors is how densely the grass blades are growing. If your lawn was recently established using turf rolls the grass blades are likely to be growing close together anyway so the best thing to do is it carry on fertilising and overseeding the lawn at the appropriate intervals to maintain the thickness. If your lawn has not yet reached an adequate level of thickness, you can also encourage it by regularly overseeding and watering, which will help to fill gaps amongst the grass blades and maintain a good level of thickness.

A lack of fertilisation and or lack of watering in hot weather conditions can contribute to inadequate levels of thickness. Therefore, it always helps to water as often as possible during dry weather in the growing season, as well as fertilising at the appropriate times. Doing so will encourage the delivery of nutrients to the lawn and encourage it to grow and become thicker.

Another factor, which can impact the thickness of the lawn, is shade; if your garden has many shaded areas you might find that in those places the lawn is thinner. The lack of sunlight makes it more challenging for the grass to photosynthesise and therefore in shady areas, the grass blades are likely to be weaker and thinner. This problem can be overcome with a combination of using a specialised type of shade-tolerant grass seed to overseed the shaded areas and making efforts to reduce the number of shaded areas. For example, a large amount of shade in the garden is due to overgrown trees and shrubbery; cutting these back to allow more sunlight in can have an amazing effect on the lawn.

Weeds, moss, and thatch can also contribute to brown patches or uneven thickness in the lawn, taking space and nutrients away from the grass and then drying out to leave the lawn with patches of brown decomposing weeds and moss.

Dealing with grass clippings

Some lawnmowers (including ride-on and cylinder mowers) have grass collectors, some are mulching lawnmowers and others are side or rear discharge lawnmowers, for this purpose I will refer to these as discharge lawnmowers. A collecting lawnmower picks up the grass clippings in a collection box, meaning that you can simply empty the box into a compost bin or garden waste bin and the lawn will be free of grass clippings. Some collector mowers also offer mulching or discharge options where the clippings are diverted from entering the collection box and either circulated around the blades again or, discharged through a discharge chute. A mulching lawnmower does not have a collection box; it circulates the grass

clippings around the mower blades multiple times ensuring that they are cut into extra fine pieces. The clippings are then discharged back onto the lawn and act as a natural fertiliser; however, the clippings may still sit on top of the lawn. Finally, a discharge lawnmower does not have a collection box either; instead, it has either a side or rear discharge chute, where the grass clippings are simply discharged back onto the lawn. Some collecting lawnmowers also offer a discharge option and some discharge lawnmowers offer a mulching option. To confuse you further, some discharge ride-on mowers offer a collecting option.

Discharge lawnmowers are effective if you just wish to cut grass and not have to deal with grass clippings. However, if you wish to maintain a lawn, discharging grass clippings is a bad idea as they are likely to sit on top of the lawn. In my experience, the best choice for a well-maintained lawn is a collecting lawnmower, as you will definitely need to collect your clippings at the first cut of the year and also on occasions when the lawn has been mowed less frequently than once a week. Using a mulching or discharge lawnmower to cut abnormally long grass is a very bad idea, as it causes clumps of grass clippings to be deposited on your lawn that, if left there, will rot and contribute to moss and bare patches. Collecting lawnmowers that come with a mulching function should only really be used in the summer if the lawn is consistently being mowed once a week. If you are using a grass collector, you should ensure that you have a suitable method for disposing of grass clippings, this could be a compost heap or bin, alternatively, if you have a relatively small lawn, therefore fewer grass clippings, many councils offer a garden waste bin.

Stripes

Stripes have been a popular feature in British gardens for countless years. Many people find a perfectly striped lawn aesthetically pleasing, this is because it provides the entire garden with a neat and tidy look and is useful at hiding imperfections such as bumps in the lawn. The most

common pattern for lawn stripping is the standard straight lines that run up and down the lawn, however, it is possible to mow just about any pattern into a lawn including the 'checkerboard' or 'diamond' patterns. A striped lawn effect is created by the grass blades, laying in a certain direction, with sunlight reflecting on them. The correct way to create this effect is to mow the lawn at a relatively high setting and use a lawnmower with either an in-built roller (usually a 'rear roller mower') or a striping kit, some ride-on mowers have rollers attached to the cutting deck or the grass collector. This will ensure that the grass blades are bent in the direction that the lawnmower is going in.

Hence it is crucial that the lawn is mowed correctly by moving the lawnmower up and down the lawn in neat lines parallel with the longest side of the lawn (or in the correct direction for whatever pattern you may be creating. The incorrect method of striping a lawn is to mow the lawn at a very low setting and have the lawnmower blades cut into the bottom of the grass. This creates a similar-looking effect to proper striping but using this method is very harmful to the lawn; it doesn't look as good as proper stripes and could potentially destroy the lawn by causing scalping and bare patches.

Proper lawn stripes are well visible for approximately one week however this can be affected by a large amount of foot traffic, windy weather or the use of a leaf blower or leaf vacuum on the lawn in the autumn months. In these cases, the stripes can last for a much shorter amount of time. If you have a thick, well-watered, green lawn the stripes are likely to be more visible.

The natural lawn

Whilst some people enjoy a neatly manicured lawn, others may wish to have a more natural-looking wildlife-friendly lawn, or maybe both at the same time. A natural or wildlife lawn has multiple benefits: these include not having the chore of lawnmowing regularly, creating biodiversity by encouraging wildflowers and encouraging wildlife, such as wild birds and bees to inhabit the garden. Depending on the size of your lawn and on your preferences, you could have a wildlife border or an entire wildlife lawn.

A wildlife border can be created in just about any sized garden; the idea is that a strip along an edge of the lawn (the wider the better) is left to grow. This way you can have your everyday well-manicured lawn in one part of the garden and a colourful meadow in another. Wildflowers and tall grass will appear colourful and pleasant whilst encouraging wildlife including birds and insects to inhabit the garden. Alternatively, if you have a large garden, or perhaps a paddock, you may wish to create a whole wildlife lawn. To do this you should carry out the same process as with a wildlife border except on a larger scale. Having a larger area means that more wildflowers can grow and more wildlife can be attracted.

You can encourage wildflowers to inhabit your natural lawn by sowing various wildflower seeds (you can buy mixtures) or planting bulbs in that section of the garden and allowing them to grow undisturbed.

If you are establishing a wildlife meadow or border from scratch, you may wish to use a mixture of grass seed that includes lower maintenance grasses such as ryegrass. This requires less care and maintenance and can just be left to grow, meaning it does not need to be watered and fertilised regularly to look good.

If you are creating a wildlife lawn, you may wish to mow some grass paths through it, these paths are fine to be the same width as your lawnmower. The idea is that you mow the grass paths once a week in the growing season and leave the rest of the lawn to grow. This way you have a completely natural wildlife-friendly path running through the tall grass. This means that you can have a leisurely stroll through your garden to admire the wildflowers without having to wade through tall grass and the presence of the paths demonstrates that yours is an intended natural lawn and not just a neglected one.

If you wish, you can cut the grass in the natural lawn once a year, it is best to either use a scythe, or a tall grass mulching deck – compatible with certain ride-on-mowers. It is best to mow in mid-autumn (October) as this is when the wildflowers will have completed their cycle and gone to seed. Long grass should never be cut in the winter as there may be nests belonging to wildlife such as hibernating hedgehogs that would be harmed if the grass were cut in the winter.

General garden maintenance

The main topic of this book is lawn maintenance, however, it is worth putting effort into keeping other parts of your garden neat and tidy too, as this will have a knock-on effect on how the lawn looks in the garden.

If you have any hedging or shrubbery in or around your lawn, you should ensure that it is always looking its best. With hedging, in particular, you can make it look well-manicured by regularly (every month) trimming it back. In the growing season, hedging is going to grow, causing small twigs and branches to stick out unevenly, these can easily be removed using a hedge cutter, or shears, to trim them back giving a smooth finish. Doing so can work wonders

on how the garden looks as a whole. This guidance is suitable for many hedging plants, but you should make sure that doing this does not harm your particular hedge before trimming.

Another part of the garden worth maintaining is flowerbeds. Many gardens have flowerbeds next to the lawn. If you do, it is worth ensuring that the flowerbed is free of weeds. You should weed flowerbeds approximately once every two weeks in the growing season. If appropriate, you should also ensure that the border between the lawn and flowerbed is tidy, I have explained this process in more detail in the 'Lawn edging' section of chapter five. Having a weed-free and well-edged flowerbed will also improve the appearance of both the lawn and the garden as a whole.

Finally, if you have a concrete or paved path or patio in your garden, it is worth making sure that it is kept clean. In any garden, a path or patio is likely to accumulate sediment such as moss, weeds, mud, leaves, dust and grass clippings after lawn mowing. This can be removed easily and will make the entire garden look neater and tidier. For moss or weeds growing in cracks or between paving slabs, you should use a purpose-made weed killer that can be sprayed directly onto the weeds or moss. This will cause the weeds or moss to dry up and die; then you can use a tool such as a patio knife to scrape them out.

Alternatively, you could use a weed burner, this is a piece of equipment designed to set weeds on fire and burn them out of your path or patio. Weed burners are available in both electric and gas models, an advantage of the electric models is that they do not use a flame and are therefore safer to operate, whereas an advantage of gas models is that you do not have to deal with an electrical wire. For other debris or sediment, you can either use a normal broom or even a leaf blower to clear it up. If you have a paved path or patio, you may also wish to jet wash it once or twice a year, as this will remove moss, weeds and any other tough sediment. You could purchase or hire a jet washer and do this yourself, however, you can also employ the services of a professional to do it.

Pets and Patches

If you do not have any dogs this will not affect you. However, many people do have dogs as pets, as lovely as dogs are, their urine can cause brown patches on the lawn. There is no good way to avoid this, especially if the offending dog is a beloved family pet. Unless you are an outstanding dog trainer and can teach your dog to use a lavatory, they still need to perform essential tasks in the garden. Therefore, possible ways to combat this problem include banishing dogs from the lawn and creating a fenced-off dog exercise area in another part of the garden or identifying the dog's most commonly used areas for urination and generously watering them regularly in an attempt to wash away the urine. If a brown patch is already present, you may need to re-seed that part of the lawn.

Other nuisances

Whilst most wildlife should be preserved and protected, some specific creatures are just an absolute nuisance to the lawn. These include moles, foxes and badgers, so it is best to deter them from the garden without harming them.

Firstly, moles can damage a lawn by creating unpleasant molehills on the surface, causing bare patches. They can also make the lawn uneven when their underground tunnels collapse causing uneven lines to appear in the lawn. One way of eliminating moles from the garden is by using natural deterrents, these include 'vegetative barriers'; plants such as daffodils can repel moles.

Foxes can also be a nuisance to the lawn; foxes dig shallow holes in the surface of the lawn when looking for earthworms to consume. This is usually a seasonal problem as the worms will be closer to the surface when the ground is moist, for example, in the spring. If you have a beautiful lawn with soft good quality topsoil (more worms), you are more likely to become a victim. A lawn can be destroyed by foxes as the holes can cover large surface areas, meaning that often the lawn has to be completely re-turfed. If this affects you, it is best to first discourage foxes from your garden by securing food waste bins and/or using suitable fencing.

Finally, badgers also dig similar shallow holes in the lawn as foxes, thus destroying the lawn and meaning new turf has to be laid. In some areas of the United Kingdom, it is illegal to kill or harm badgers, whilst in others, it is legal for individuals with certain licences. Irrespective of what the regulations are in your area, I would advise against killing or harming badgers. Instead, you could use other methods such as temporarily laying chicken wire on the ground over certain parts of the lawn, this will prevent the badgers (also works with foxes) from digging holes without harming the animals in any way.

Leaf clearance

It might seem surprising but clearing leaves from the lawn is a vital part of lawn care. If there are mature deciduous trees anywhere near your lawn, in the autumn your lawn will likely have a vast amount of leaves deposited upon it. Any deposition of leaves or other organic matter in large quantities on the lawn is likely to be harmful. The leaf matter is likely to start rotting and decomposing on top of the grass, covering the grass from sunlight and making it rot too, causing bare patches.

The worst types of leaves to be deposited on the lawn are acidic ones. For example, oak tree leaves are very acidic and take an exceptionally long time to decompose. If these leaves are left on top of the lawn over winter, they can eliminate all the grass underneath them. This causes brown and/or bare patches in the lawn, as well as depositing acid in the soil where they were resting over the winter. Even if you try to overseed after having removed the leaves, it is unlikely that grass will grow on those patches for the next couple of years.

Therefore, it is essential that leaves are removed from the lawn as quickly as possible. There is an approximate four-week period, usually between the end of November and the beginning of December, (this can vary on weather conditions), when deciduous

trees are dropping their leaves most frequently. This is when clearing leaves should be your highest priority. In this period, it is most effective to clear leaves at least once a week, every week, until there are no leaves left on deciduous trees.

There are several different ways to go about clearing leaves; if you have a relatively small lawn it is fine to simply rake up and dispose of the leaves, however, is your lawn is larger than a quarter of an acre you may wish to consider investing in a leaf blower, a leaf vacuum, or even a ride-on mower with a powered grass collector.

On average these machines are very effective, however, as with all garden machines, effectiveness and reliability can vary depending on make and model so make sure that you acquire the right one for you. When disposing of leaves bear in mind that leaves, especially if they are acidic, can take several years to decompose in a compost heap. Depending on the quantity, I would recommend methods such as, burning the leaves (if appropriate) or disposing of them in a garden waste bin if you have one.

Compost heaps or bins

As discussed in earlier chapters, for garden tasks such as lawnmowing you are likely to require a method to dispose of garden waste such as grass clippings. People with relatively small gardens may be able to dispose of their garden waste through means such as council provided garden waste bins. However, if you have a relatively large garden with a lot of garden waste, or just wish to use one of the most eco-friendly methods, a compost heap or bin might be the right solution.

The difference between a compost bin and a compost heap is the fact that a compost bin is usually a plastic container similar in size to a water butt and a compost heap is a pile of garden waste on the way to becoming compost, this is often contained within a concrete or wooden structure.

If you have a relatively small garden you may wish to use a compost bin, these can be acquired from most hardware shops and online retailers. A compost bin will provide you with a discrete and contained way to dispose of garden waste. Alternatively, if you have a relatively large garden with a lot of garden waste, you may wish to create a larger compost heap. To maximise efficiency and make it more aesthetically pleasing, you may wish to erect a concrete or wooden structure around it. One of such structures is usually a square container occupying approximately one cube metre. It should ideally be erected using either old pallets or planks of wood (wire netting also works) supported by large posts in each corner. In most cases it should be a box with four walls (a pallet per side), however, if you are using a ride-on mower to mow your lawn, it is better to only build three sides so you can reverse into the compost heap and empty the collector of the ride-on mower.

The most effective way to make compost is by allowing all of the garden waste to decompose for about a year before using the compost. Six months into the year, it is worth using a fork to remove and re-stack the compost, ensuring that it rots evenly throughout. An effective way of going about this is to have two compost bins or a larger heap with two compartments. The idea is that in one year you will only deposit garden waste in one bin or compartment and the next year you will only deposit waste in the other (whilst the waste in the first one is decomposing).

After one year of decomposing, the first bin or compartment can be emptied and used for depositing new waste, whilst the second one is decomposing and so on. This will ensure that all the garden waste is sufficiently decomposed to be used as compost and that you always have available space to deposit garden waste.

Regardless of whether it is a bin or a heap, the garden waste should be deposited in a certain place, where it decomposes over time and becomes compost, which can then be spread in the appropriate

places around the garden. If the waste in the compost heap is particularly dry, it is worth using water from a hose-pipe to moisten it, thus speeding up the rotting process.

The compost making process can be made more effective by introducing compost accelerators. They speed up the breakdown of the garden waste, making the composting process faster and more effective. Alternatively, you can use compost worms. These are usually Tiger worms (Eisenia Fetida) these work similarly to a compost accelerator, quickly processing the compost, except they do this in the most organic way possible. Both compost accelerator and compost worms are available from many garden centres and internet retailers.

Glossary

Cutting deck[1]

The enclosed part of a lawnmower where the blades are located, the width of the cutting deck usually determines the cutting width of the lawnmower.

Grass blades[2]

Blade shaped leaves of the grass plant.

PTO[3]

Power take-off.

Scalping[4]

A far too low height setting causing the lawnmower blades to cut into the surface of the soil leaving bare patches in place of the grass.

Foot traffic[5]

An area of the lawn being regularly trodden on by people and or animals.

Inches/Feet[6/7]

Unit of measurement 1 inch = 2.54 centimetres, 1 foot = 12 inches/30.48 centimetres.

About the author

Martin Sallai is a part-time gardener, lawn and machinery enthusiast and blogger. He wrote this book during the coronavirus lockdown of 2020 alongside his studies and gardening work. Martin lives with his family in rural Kent.

For more information visit:

- Blog: lawnsandmowers.wordpress.com
- Instagram: @lawnsandmowers
- Facebook: Lawns and Mowers UK

Acknowledgements

I would like to express my deepest thanks to my friends and family members for all their help giving feedback on the book and helping to publish it. I would also like to thank Sharon Higgins for her help with proofreading the book. Furthermore, I would like to thank Jackie Harris and Karen Wright for helping me develop my skills in writing and encouraging me to succeed with this book. I would like to thank Mark and Amanda of M&A Brown & Sons Ltd for all of their help with the illustrations of certain machinery. Finally, thanks to Jonathan Temples for the cover and Anikó Duló for the internal design.

Picture credits

6 Pixabay: Clayton800; 8 Freepik: Welcomia; 11 Freepik: wavebreakmedia.com; 21 Freepik: goffkein; 23 Dreamstime: Roman Milert; 25 Freepik: freepik; 27 Pixabay: Silberkugel66; 30 Dreamstime: Bodgan Hoda; 31 Freepik: serg60; 33 Pixabay: titosoft; 34 Dreamstime: Dean Clarke (top), Robin Gentry (bottom); 36 Unsplash: tekton_ tools; 38-39 Freepik: Welcomia; 40 Freepik: freepik (top), volodymyr_vorona (middle), alexandrgrant (bottom); 41 Freepik: gutaper; 42 Pixabay: Dylan Garton (top), Freepik: zurijeta (bottom), 43 Freepik: zurijeta (top), Pixabay: bluebudge (bottom); 44 Unsplash: Gabriel Jimenez (bottom); 45 Pixabay: mounsey (top), Unsplash: Ochir-Erdene Ozunmedeg (bottom); 46-47 Freepik: Peangdao; 48 Dreamstime: Taran Schatz (top), Graham Corney (bottom); 47 Deamstime: lamporpla; 50 Freepik: freepik; 51 Pixabay: Eugene_Brennan; 52-53 Pixabay: MrsBrown; 55 Freepik: mikrokon; 58 Dreamstime: Pix569; 59 Unsplash: Louis Hansel; 60 Pixabay: thechance (top), Freepik: Welcomia (bottom); 61 Pixabay: josephredfield; 62-63 Freepik: 4045; 64 Freepik: freepik; 65 Dreamstime: Anujit Singkham; 68 Freepik: user8686449; 70-71 Freepik: Ilovehz; 72 Dreamstime: Alexander Raths; 75 Freepik: vh-studio; 77 Freepik: freepik; 79 Freepik: jcomp; 80-81 Freepik: Photoangel; 83 Freepik: user14977096; 84 Freepik: vh-studio (top); user11844481 (bottom); 85 Pixabay: paulbr75; 88 Pexels: Mina-Marie Michell; 89 Pixabay: RonPorter; 90 Pixabay: Couleur (top); 91 Pixabay: PhotoMIX-Company; 92 Pixabay: Krzysztof Jaracz; 93 Dreamstime: Smileus; 94 Freepik: mari.zaro; 97 Freepik: Bedneyimages; 98 Freepik: Welcomia; 101 Pixabay: Blende12 (Gerhard G.); 13-19, 26 Amanda and Mark of M&A Brown & Sons.

Disclaimer

Lightning Source UK Ltd.
Milton Keynes UK
UKHW021450271120
374134UK00008B/61